IT DON'T MEAN NOTHIN'

Terry John Care

BROADWAY PLAY PUBLISHING INC
New York
www.broadwayplaypublishing.com
info@broadwayplaypublishing.com

Cover photo by John Gomez

First edition: May 2022
I S B N: 978-0-88145-931-9

Book design: Marie Donovan
Page make-up: Adobe InDesign
Typeface: Palatino

CHARACTERS & SETTING

FRANK WEST, *a man in his early 70s*

BETTY WEST, FRANK's *third and current wife, in her mid-60s*

ROB WEST, FRANK's *son from his first marriage, in his late 40s*

CINDY WEST, ROB's *wife, in her mid-40s*

MELLOW WEST, ROB's *daughter, 19*

PEACE WEST, ROB's *daughter, 17*

ALPHONSO "WILDCAT" GOMEZ, FRANK's *army buddy, in his early 70s*

"BANGKOK" BILLY HUSTAD, FRANK's *army buddy, in his early 70s*

JOEY "HARDROCK" BROOKS, FRANK's *army buddy, in his early 70s*

The entire play is set in the living room of FRANK *and* BETTY WEST's *aging house in the small town of Oil Ridge, Kansas.*

Time: April of 2021

ACT ONE

Scene 1

(Setting: The living room of the small, older house owned by FRANK *and* BETTY WEST. *The house is roughly one-hundred years old, built sturdily during the boom days of Oil Ridge, Kansas. Still, the dull, white ceiling slants slightly downward from left to right. The beaten oak floor is amply covered with three large, worn, patterned carpets. There is a screened fireplace in the mid-point of the rear wall, and twin built- in, mostly empty bookshelves on either side of it extend upward to the ceiling. Between the bookshelves and floor lamps are matching windows with the Venetian blinds raised. Sunlight from the April afternoon generously blesses the room. The heavy oak front door is in the left wall, and another window, blinds up and the same size as the others, is halfway between the door and the left wall corner. An open hallway entrance in the right wall leads to three bedrooms, two bathrooms, and a kitchen, none of which is visible to the audience. In the room's center, matching love seat and sofa, covered in imitation leather, face each other at right angles to the audience. A brown coffee table, obviously of imitation wood, stands before the sofa, and matching end tables are beside each recliner. The coffee table is covered with a half-dozen out-of-date magazines. Framed family photographs, black-and-white as well as color, stand on the fireplace mantel. Cheap reproductions of still-life paintings hang here and there. The overall impression is that of a functional though unremarkable house.)*

(At rise: FRANK WEST *is standing before and facing the window near the front door, lost in thought. He is dressed in denims and a blue pullover sports shirt that extends a little below his thin waist.* BETTY WEST *is leaning over the coffee table, her back to* FRANK, *arranging the magazines. She, too, is dressed in denims and a pullover shirt. Her hair is short, gray, and not styled, a concession to the inevitability of aging. She might be considered acceptably overweight, and her otherwise attractive face has bulged over time.)*

BETTY: *(Standing and surveying the magazine arrangement)* Nothing more to do now but wait. Did you hang up your towel? They'll want to see the house.

FRANK: *(Continuing to gaze out the window)* They're not going to care about a damn towel.

BETTY: *(Approaches* FRANK *and, from behind him, rests her arms on his shoulders.)* You don't have any idea how much I want this day to be special for you. I just want you to make a good impression on your friends.

FRANK: *(Turns toward* BETTY *whose arms fall to her sides. He is suddenly agitated.)* I'll say it once more. They're not my friends. Hell, I haven't seen them since '68. They were my buddies.

BETTY: Sorry. I meant to say buddies, but I still don't understand the difference.

FRANK: *(Silent a moment before responding. He is still agitated.)* I can't explain it. Friends do stuff together. Buddies...well, it was an Army thing. I can't explain it.

BETTY: *(Attempting enthusiasm.)* Which one are you most excited about seeing? You must have had a favorite buddy.

FRANK: *(Shrugs as he makes his way to the recliner nearest the sofa)* I guess it'll be good to see both of them. Is that what you wanted me to say?

BETTY: *(Taken aback, she sits on the end of the sofa closest to* FRANK.*)* Honey, I'm just trying to help you get ready for this. I didn't even know you'd been to Vietnam until you called that waiter a goddamn gook. You never said a thing until I saw all the stitches and scars down your back and butt.

FRANK: Well, that's just the way everyone talked over there.

BETTY: Let's just concentrate on having a good time with your old buddies. I'm sure they're as nervous as you are.

FRANK: I'm not nervous. I'm just...I don't know what I am.

(The front door suddenly opens. ROB WEST, FRANK's *middle age son, steps inside. He is a few pounds overweight and dressed casually.* CINDY WEST, ROB's *wife of about the same age, follows. She is squat and dressed in a sweater and jeans too tight for her.)*

ROB: *(Smiling broadly)* Hi, Dad. Hi, Betty. Just dropped in to meet Dad's fellow storm troopers. They're not here yet?

BETTY: Any minute now.

CINDY: We brought the girls. Okay if we bring them in?

BETTY: *(Stands, glances at* FRANK, *then addresses* ROB *and* CINDY.*)* Sure. It's not everyday that Frank gets to play grandpa.

*(*CINDY *exits out the front door.* ROB *approaches* FRANK *who stands. They hug warmly.)*

ROB: It's going to be a fun time, Dad. Long overdue. You guys went through hell. *(He hugs* BETTY.*)* Thanks for doing all the work, Betty. And all because of that crazy email. What's his name again?

BETTY: Alphonso Gomez, but your dad says he was called Wildcat.

ROB: *(Laughs)* Wildcat. Wow! What did they call you, Dad?

FRANK: *(Subdued)* I forget.

ROB: Well, I'm sure Wildcat will remember.

BETTY: I need to go see if the steaks have thawed out. I can make sandwiches for the girls, Rob, if they're hungry now.

ROB: What growing girls aren't always hungry?

(BETTY exits stage right. ROB sits on the sofa and FRANK returns to his recliner.) You're up for this, right, Dad? I've been to two high school reunions and they were a blast.

(CINDY and daughters MELLOW and PEACE enter through the front door. The girls, like CINDY, are dressed in sweatshirt, jeans, and athletic shoes. MELLOW is well on her way to obesity, while PEACE is abnormally thin. Each has a cell phone tucked into a rear pocket. They stop as though awaiting instructions.)

CINDY: Say hi to your grandfather, girls. He's a big war hero. You should always remember that.

(MELLOW and PEACE mumble something that resembles greetings.)

PEACE: *(Steps forward and kisses FRANK on the forehead.)* Love ya, Grandpa.

FRANK: *(Smiles a little as he reaches for PEACE's hand.)* Love you, too.

CINDY: Your grandfather won a Purple Heart, kids. Did he ever tell you that?

(MELLOW *and* PEACE, *ignoring* CINDY, *pull out their cell phones and begin texting.*) Someday when he's up to it I'm sure he'll tell you all about it.

ROB: *(Laughing)* Wrong place, wrong time. That's all he ever tells me.

FRANK: *(Clearly wishing to change the subject.)* So how's work?

ROB: Samo-samo.

CINDY: I'm going to go help Betty in the kitchen. I'll have the girls set up the chairs and tables in the backyard. It's going to be a great barbecue, Frank. *(She kisses* FRANK's *cheek.)* Rob, you just stay right here and talk with your father. He's one of a kind. *(She heads toward stage right.)* Come on, girls.

(MELLOW *and* PEACE *follow in single file, continuing to work their cell phones.* FRANK *returns to the recliner, and* ROB *takes the sofa.)*

FRANK: Want a beer or something? Betty bought a bunch of it.

ROB: Later, maybe, after your friends get here. Betty told me you actually haven't been in touch with them for years.

FRANK: Decades.

ROB: So how exactly did this happen, this reunion?

FRANK: *(Taking his time before answering, looking straight ahead and far away.)* Betty did the whole thing.

ROB: And it started with an email from this Wildcat character?

FRANK: I guess some people have nothing better to do than go looking on their goddamn computers for people from way back when. Anyway, he found my name and old email address on the Green Grow Nursery website. My picture, too. So he sent me an email there, and the nursery sent it here. Betty answered him, not me. I left that place three years ago. Why the hell would they still have me on their website?

ROB: I'm glad they did.

FRANK: People should just let the past be the past. I told Betty to just let it go but she answered him anyway.

ROB: You make it sound like you don't really want to see Wildcat or the guy coming with him.

FRANK: I can't explain it.

CINDY: *(Enters from stage right with a demure* PEACE *following.)* Frank, Peace here wants to know how you won your Purple Heart. What it was like and all.

ROB: *(Recognizing* FRANK'*s discomfort,* ROB *stands.)* We can talk about all that later when everyone gets here. I'm sure there will be lots of stories today.

CINDY: Well, maybe you've heard it all before but his granddaughters…

FRANK: *(Quickly coming to his feet)* Wrong place, wrong time, if you really need to know. Simple as that. That's the whole goddamn story. And you don't win a Purple Heart like it's some kind of goddamn school prize.

CINDY: *(Aghast, she hesitates.)* I'm sorry, Frank. Well, It can wait. We'll be in the kitchen. Come on, Peace. *(Starts toward stage right.)*

FRANK: Just a minute. *(Awkwardly.)* Sometimes I…well, I don't know how to say it. *(He gently places a hand on* PEACE'*s shoulder.)* I'm sorry this sweet young thing heard me use language like that. I'm sure everything will be just fine.

*(*CINDY *and* PEACE *exit stage right.)*

ROB: *(Rests a hand on* FRANK'*s shoulder)* Sit back down, Dad. If I'd had any idea this thing was going to upset you so much maybe I would have said something to Betty.

(FRANK *slowly returns to the recliner, and* ROB *to the sofa.*)

FRANK: When Betty told me what she was up to I didn't think much about it. I guess I was thinking it might be fun to see old Wildcat again, him and Bangkok Billy. Now, I don't know.

ROB: Bangkok Billy?

FRANK: (*Grunts with a smile*) He was in second squad, too. He went to Bangkok on R and R and came back with the clap. We never let him forget it. Wildcat found him on his computer, too. Turns out they live near each other down in Oklahoma someplace and didn't even know it.

ROB: Dad, do you have any idea what a great story this is? Three guys from Vietnam getting together more than fifty years later. Wow. We should call the newspaper.

FRANK: No need for that.

ROB: Who else was in your squad, if you don't mind me asking?

FRANK: (*Shrugs*) Guys came and went. We had one guy who got it through the head the first day he was with us. I never knew his name.

ROB: So how long were you with Wildcat and Billy?

FRANK: (*Shrugs again*) It all runs together. Wildcat was already in-country when I got there. Billy got there a month or so after me. I lasted a whole hundred and twenty-seven days, so I guess we were together for a few months before we all got hit.

ROB: You all got hit the same day?

FRANK: (*Pauses, obviously unhappy with himself for revealing details*) Yeah. Same day.

ROB: How bad did you guys get it?

FRANK: *(Hesitates)* Billy got the worst of it. He lost one leg B K and the other A K. Maybe some other stuff. I heard about it later when I was in the hospital in San Francisco. I think they sent him to Walter Reed.

ROB: B K?

FRANK: Below the knee. A K is above the knee. I learned all that stuff that year in rehab.

ROB: *(Shakes his head in disbelief)* And Wildcat?

FRANK: Mostly his guts.

ROB: And I'll bet you still won't tell me exactly what happened to your group?

FRANK: We were a squad, goddamnit, not a group.

ROB: Sorry.

FRANK: *(Leans toward* ROB *and looks directly into his eyes.)* You need to understand something, and this is all I'm going to say about it. In 1968 everybody got hit. Tet Offensive and all that, though you probably don't know what the hell I'm talking about. I'd only been in the field a week when our point man was K I A. Killed in action. That's when I realized I really was in Nam with no way out, not for three hundred and sixty-five days. So I started counting the days. Boy, did we count the days, even though nobody expected to make it all the way to three hundred and sixty-five. All we wanted was not to get killed, and not to get our balls and dicks blown off. Losing an arm or leg or getting shot to pieces, that was okay. *(Stands quickly, then just as quickly returns to the recliner.)* Damnit! I never should have let Betty do this.

ROB: *(Stares admiringly at* FRANK*)* That's the most you've ever told me, Dad.

FRANK: *(Shaking his head)* I should have told her to forget the whole idea.

ROB: I'm sure she thought she was doing something special for you.

FRANK: I don't need anybody doing anything for me. That was the problem with your mother, always doing stuff I didn't want, and telling me she was only doing it for me. You know what finally did it between her and me?

ROB: It doesn't matter anymore, Dad.

FRANK: She turned Catholic all of a sudden, just a few months after your sister was born when you were still a toddler. I wouldn't go to mass with her. So one day after work I came home to our apartment and found her and a priest waiting for me. She'd brought him there to convert me. It took me ten seconds to get rid of that faggot son-of-a-bitch. She started screaming she'd only done it for my own good. I'm sure you don't remember it but we split up right after that.

ROB: Dad, she's been dead for eleven years.

FRANK: She never told you about that?

ROB: *(Suddenly upset)* Actually, she told me once she had to leave you because of your drinking. She said Vietnam had messed you up so bad nobody could ever save you.

FRANK: *(Grunts sarcastically)* Well, believe what you want.

(The doorbell rings. FRANK stares at the door while ROB waits for FRANK to make a move. The doorbell rings a second time.)

BETTY: *(Off)* Are you both deaf?

(BETTY enters in a trot from stage right and heads for the front door. She dramatically pulls open the door, and stares

at a figure not visible to the audience. FRANK *and* ROB *stand slowly, facing the door.* BETTY *addresses the figure at the door.)*

BETTY: You've got to be Wildcat! You get in here!

*(*WILDCAT, *a tall, heavyset man in denims and sport shirt steps into the room. His soft, enlarged gut droops over his waistline. He is wearing a dark blue baseball cap that reads in yellow above the bill "VIETNAM VETERAN." He smiles broadly while awkwardly coming to attention and saluting* BETTY.)*

WILDCAT: Specialist Gomez reporting as ordered, ma'am.

BETTY: *(Stretching onto her toes,* BETTY *tightly hugs Wildcat, grabs his hands, and steps back.)* The legend himself! Oh, this is wonderful.

WILDCAT: Hope you don't mind I'm not wearing one of those COVID masks. I got one in the car.

BETTY: *(Laughs)* This is Kansas, Wildcat. They shoot you for wearing a mask.

WILDCAT: Yes, ma'am. Same in Oklahoma.

BETTY: *(She steps aside and waves an open arm toward* FRANK.)* He's standing right there, Wildcat. Your old buddy.

FRANK: It's been a long time, Alphonso. Nice to see you.

*(*WILDCAT *pauses before approaching* FRANK. *He extends his hand, withdraws it, then smothers* FRANK *in a hug.* FRANK *reservedly hugs* WILDCAT *in return.* WILDCAT *relaxes his hug, and joyfully shakes* FRANK *by the shoulders and laughs.)*

WILDCAT: My god! I think I'd recognize you anywhere, Cherryboy. You look a hell of a lot younger than me, I'll say that much. I'm just an old fat guy.

ROB: *(Laughing)* Cherryboy?

FRANK: *(He nods toward* ROB.*)* This is my son, Alphonso. And here's Betty, your email pen pal, in the flesh.

ROB: Cherryboy?

*(*WILDCAT *belts a laugh, and shakes hands with* ROB:*)*

WILDCAT: We called your dad Cherryboy. We were always kidding him about being a virgin. I can see he got that problem fixed.

BETTY: How about a beer, Wildcat? It must have been a long drive.

WILDCAT: Damn straight!

*(*BETTY *exits stage right.* FRANK *motions for* WILDCAT *to sit on the sofa.* ROB *sits beside* WILDCAT, *and* FRANK *returns to the recliner.)*

WILDCAT: Last time I saw you, Cherryboy, I was all torn up and trying to carry Billy on my back to that dustoff. I bet I was a mess. I remember screaming like crazy.

ROB: Dustoff?

WILDCAT: That's what we called those medical evacuation choppers, the ones with the big red crosses painted on them. You see them in the movies. *(Laughs)* Hell, Cherryboy, you never told your boy here about dustoffs?

FRANK: *(Shrugs)* I heard in the hospital that Brenner got it a month later. Bouncing betty. He lost both legs.

ROB: Bouncing betty?

WILDCAT: *(He faces* ROB.*)* I can see your old man hasn't told you a damn thing. A bouncing betty was the worst kind of booby trap there was. You step on one of those sons-of-bitches and it pops out of the ground and goes off right about waist high. Rips your legs off, among other things. *(Laughs)* Jesus, I hope your mom wasn't named after one of those things.

ROB: She's not my mom.

WILDCAT: Oh? Wife number two, Cherryboy?

FRANK: *(He raises his right hand and displays three fingers.)* Number three.

WILDCAT: Goddamn. Well, I've had a couple myself. The last one walked out twenty years ago. No number three for me.

*(*BETTY *returns with two cans of beer and hands one to* WILDCAT *and one to* ROB:)*

BETTY: I am so glad you're here, Wildcat. Frank won't admit it but he knows this will be a wonderful day for all of us. He never sees anybody. He says he'd rather spend time with marigolds than with people. Now, you men just sit here and talk while I go take care of things. *(She exits right.)*

WILDCAT: *(Laughs again)* You got a good woman this time, Cherryboy.

FRANK: Nobody's called me that since Nam.

WILDCAT: Betty told me you got sent to that Army hospital out there in San Francisco for a whole year. They sent me to Sam Houston. Billy went to Walter Reed. I wonder why the hell they split us up like that?

FRANK: No idea. Maybe different hospitals did different things.

WILDCAT: *(Looks at* FRANK *up and down)* Sure looks like you get around okay for a guy who got blown to pieces.

FRANK: You, too.

WILDCAT: You know, V A finally gave me a hundred percent. Sixty percent because my spleen got blown out and part of my stomach. My hearing is messed up a little bit, there was some other stuff, and the rest for P T S D. It took years for the bastards to see it my way. I tried twice for Agent Orange. They tested me and tested me, but they turned me down. They said I didn't have one of those diseases you have to have. What about you?

FRANK: Seventy percent.

WILDCAT: Just seventy?

FRANK: Partial loss of motion, nerve damage, some hearing loss like you.

WILDCAT: Nothing for P T S D?

FRANK: Never thought about it.

WILDCAT: *(Dumbfounded)* Never thought about it? Hell, P T S D is yours for the asking! Just go in there and tell them you have nightmares and flashbacks all the time. There's good money in it.

FRANK: I guess I always just wanted to get on with my life.

ROB: *(Slightly offended)* Dad, how come you never told me any of this? If you're entitled to it, go for it. No reason not to.

FRANK: I'm okay with what they gave me.

(WILDCAT stares at FRANK awhile. WILDCAT and ROB take a couple drinks of their beers, glance at each other, and simultaneously shake their heads.)

WILDCAT: They owe you, buddy. At least think about it. *(Pauses)* Heh, why don't we take a minute and toast second squad, those who came before us and those who came after us. *(He raises his beer.)* Where's your beer, Frank?

FRANK: I don't drink anymore.

WILDCAT: Oh, I get it. I've had a few D U Is myself, if you want to know the truth. So has Bangkok Billy.

FRANK: *(Defensively)* I didn't say I've ever had a D U I.

WILDCAT: Well, drinking is just part of the package for guys like us. I even got fired once for being drunk. You just have to pace yourself is all. Remember that night when Rocky Foster and Sergeant Southland got drunk on L Z Osage and got into that fight?

FRANK: *(Becoming impatient)* Not really.

ROB: L Z Osage?

WILDCAT: *(Turns to* ROB*)* Landing Zone Osage. A landing zone was like a fort on a hill. They were called firebases and we had them all over Nam. The army had bullshit names for them. *(He returns to* FRANK.*)* Hell, how could you forget something like that? In fact, you were one of the guys that broke it up. Foster bit off Southland's nipple. *(Faces* ROB*)* He never told you about that?

ROB: *(Transfixed)* Not really.

WILDCAT: Imagine that.

FRANK: *(Anxious to change the subject)* Betty told me you said in an e-mail you're retired.

WILDCAT: Yep. I've had more than a couple retirements, actually, but this one's here to stay. Eight years now.

FRANK: She didn't tell me what you did.

WILDCAT: Handyman. You can actually do pretty good as a handyman. It's all cash so the I R S never knows. I know you worked in a nursery. I guess that's what Betty meant about you and marigolds. How were you able to dig holes and haul stuff around with all that shrapnel in you?

FRANK: I worked in the back, out of sight of everyone. Trees, bushes, flowers and sod. I watered, clipped, trimmed, and fed everything.

ROB: For nine years he did it.

WILDCAT: Sounds kind of boring.

FRANK: *(Again defensively)* It was very peaceful, Alphonso. I was nursing roses while the rest of the world was busy stomping on them.

WILDCAT: Well, whatever works. You know, I gave Betty my phone number. How come you never called me?

ROB: *(Jumps in quickly)* Dad doesn't like talking on phones, any kind of phone.

WILDCAT: Never heard that one before. Anyway, let's drink to second squad.

(WILDCAT raises his beer as does ROB. FRANK lifts his empty hand as though raising a beer.)

WILDCAT: To second squad, the meanest bastards in the valley of death.

(FRANK nods slightly in acknowledgement, while ROB nods with enthusiasm.)

WILDCAT: Wait! Wait a minute! We need to drink to Joker, the best squad leader the Army ever had. To Joker!

(WILDCAT raises his beer and ROB follows. FRANK again lifts an empty hand.)

ROB: Who's Joker?

WILDCAT: Like I said, kid, the best damn squad leader the Army ever saw. I can't count the number of times he saved our asses. Right, Frank?

FRANK: True story.

WILDCAT: *(Facing ROB)* Joker was your dad's buddy.

ROB: *(Laughs)* Joker? There must have been a reason for a name like that. *(Addressing* FRANK.*)* How come you never told me about Joker? Did he know about today?

*(*WILDCAT *awkwardly glances at* FRANK *who says nothing, then returns to* ROB:*)*

WILDCAT: He didn't make it. K I A.

ROB: *(Uncertain what to do, he stands.)* Well, I'm going to go see what the women are up to. *(Patting* WILDCAT'*s shoulder.)* Nice to meet you, Wildcat. You guys just sit right here and talk things over. *(He exits right.)*

WILDCAT: *(Waits until* ROB *is gone. He drinks while speaking with* FRANK.*)* Seems like a really good kid. So you never told him about Joker?

FRANK: *(Shakes his head dismissively)* I never had any trouble with Rob. I kept waiting for the divorce to mess him up, but it didn't happen. Lynn and I never fought in front of him, and she never said anything bad to him about me. I'll give her that.

WILDCAT: Lynn was her name?

FRANK: She was an assistant nurse at the hospital in San Francisco.

WILDCAT: Man, I saw a lot of that when I was in Sam Houston. Nurses falling in love with screwed up guys like us. A mother complex or something.

FRANK: I guess.

WILDCAT: So you just have your boy?

FRANK: He has a sister.

WILDCAT: What's—

FRANK: Roberta. And so you won't have to ask, I'll just tell you. Lynn raised her, too, and I haven't seen her since she was in high school. I don't have any idea where she is.

WILDCAT: Jesus. Doesn't Lynn know?

FRANK: Lynn passed away eleven years ago. Breast cancer. Listen, do me a big favor, Alphonso. Don't tell my son or Betty or anyone what happened when we all got hit.

WILDCAT: What? Really? You ashamed of it? No reason to be.

FRANK: Just don't. Please.

WILDCAT: Fine by me. Haven't you ever told anyone about Nam, especially about Joker? You guys were so close.

FRANK: No! *(He pauses.)* So, how was the drive coming up here?

WILDCAT: Pretty good. I had to stop in some little town for gas. I don't know why but it got me to thinking about how when we were kids and they always pumped your gas for you. Checked your oil and cleaned your windshield. Whatever happened to serving the customer?

FRANK: *(He is silent for awhile.)* What made you start looking for the guys from second squad?

WILDCAT: You mean you never wonder what happened to everybody?

FRANK: Sure I wonder. I've just never gone looking for someone like you did.

WILDCAT: *(Raises his bottle and finishes his beer.)* This might sound crazy but one day I realized that being in Nam with you and Joker and Bangkok Billy and Hardrock and all the other guys from second squad was the happiest I've ever been.

FRANK: Alphonso, we damn near got killed that day! What the hell are you talking about?

WILDCAT: I can't explain it very well. I just mean that since coming back from Nam everybody I've ever had to deal with has pretty much fucked me over. Women, the people I've worked for, my dentist even. My neighbors, too. Nobody from second squad ever did anything like that to me. We took care of each other, Cherryboy. I think about that all the time, and it just made me want to see everybody again.

FRANK: I've never thought that.

WILDCAT: Finding you was pretty hard. Bangkok Billy has Facebook so I found him first time I tried. It's funny because all this time he's been living outside Tulsa only about fifty miles from me. He's in a mobile home. Poor guy's never really had a job since the Army got rid of him. He tried clerking at a 7-Eleven, but he couldn't stand for more than five minutes. Anyway, that's what he told me.

FRANK: He was kind of messed up, but I liked him.

WILDCAT: He never even got married. I mean, what the hell are you good for with no legs? He told me they gave him a couple of those wooden legs or whatever they are, but he still uses canes. (Laughs) He said it makes him walk like Frankenstein. Anyway, he's not going to starve, not with one-hundred percent permanent. They even gave him a special car to drive. He had to do everything with his hands when he was still driving.

FRANK: He doesn't drive now?

WILDCAT: They took his license away. He kind of told me he's had a few D U Is.

FRANK: So how's he getting here?

WILDCAT: Well, guess what? (Smiles broadly.) He found old Hardrock on Facebook. He lives in Ponca City. Hardrock is driving him up here.

FRANK: *(Immediately apprehensive)* Hardrock? You mean Joey Brooks?

WILDCAT: Yeah. We're all just going to stay in a cheap motel somewhere around here.

FRANK: Betty told me only you and Billy were coming.

WILDCAT: *(Laughs)* Billy let me know late last night. It'll be good to see Hardrock, too, won't it? He got hit pretty bad that day. What was the name of that place? Binh Song? Phu Binh?

FRANK: Damn, I wish I'd known Brooks was coming, too.

WILDCAT: Like I said, I didn't find out until last night. I didn't even know Billy had found him. Heh, I can't think of the name of that place where we all got hit.

FRANK: Tri Binh.

WILDCAT: *(Grunts with a light laugh)* Tri Binh. That's it, all right. Funny how you and me remember some things about Nam the same way but not other things. Dumbass Lieutenant Stokley.

FRANK: *(Bitterly)* Stockley's the one who should have been killed.

WILDCAT: *(Shakes his head)* How the hell do you call in artillery on your own platoon? We were lucky only Joker got killed. Sometimes I wonder what he'd be doing today. I bet he'd own a couple McDonald's or something. He was a smart guy. *(Pauses)* I've always wondered about something. Was Joker already K I A when you threw him onto the dustoff? I remember him hanging over your shoulder and how tore up he was.

FRANK: It was instant. He didn't suffer.

WILDCAT: *(Nodding)* Good to know. Some guys—

FRANK: Heh, Betty bought a bunch of steaks for me to barbecue. Can you eat steaks with your guts messed up?

WILDCAT: Hell, yes. I can eat anything except gook crap. I'd eat dog food before I'd ever eat that slop.

FRANK: But your guts are okay?

WILDCAT: Oh, every few years they have to go in and cut out some more of my intestine or something. But I'm okay.

FRANK: *(Shifts nervously in his chair)* I really wish I'd known Brooks was coming. Have you talked to him yourself?

WILDCAT: No, just Billy has. But Hardrock was a part of us, man. No reason to get stressed out about it. *(Pauses)* You know, it's funny how second squad ended up living so close together and not even knowing it. You should get Facebook. Where was Joker from?

FRANK: *(Glances over his shoulder toward stage right as though hoping* BETTY *or* ROB *will return.)* A little town in Florida.

WILDCAT: Yeah. I remember now. He had a bunch of sisters, and was the only boy. *(Laughs.)* He used to joke how he loved women from the day he was born. Remember that?

FRANK: Yep.

WILDCAT: Hell, he joked about everything, especially when he was smoking weed. How many guys can say they had a squad leader who smoked weed with them? Yeah, Joker was the best.

FRANK: *(Defensively)* He only smoked it when we were standing down on a firebase, never in the boonies.

WILDCAT: *(Laughs again)* He could have been court-martialed for that. He didn't give a rat's ass. He was one of us, man. He would have died for any one of us.

(BETTY happily enters from stage right carrying a beer. She hands the beer to WILDCAT.)

BETTY: Here you go, Wildcat. Just be careful. We want everyone to be in good shape when we eat.

WILDCAT: Yes, ma'am. We'll be standing tall. Promise.

BETTY: *(Looking at FRANK)* What about you, babe? A soda?

FRANK: I'm fine.

BETTY: Then back to the kitchen I go. We're going to leave you guys alone while we take care of everything. I'm sure you have a lot of catching up to do.

FRANK: *(Starts to stand)* I can at least go grill the steaks.

BETTY: You're not going to do anything today except enjoy your friends. Your buddies, I mean. *(Exits right)*

WILDCAT: Any woman who likes beer is okay in my book. How long you two been married?

FRANK: Five years.

WILDCAT: Where the hell do you meet a woman like that?

FRANK: We both worked at the nursery. She says she fell in love with me because I talked to the flowers. *(Nodding affirmatively)* I've been very lucky.

WILDCAT: I guess you've told her about what happened to us that day at Tri Binh?

FRANK: No.

WILDCAT: No? Hell, why—

FRANK: And she knows not to ask, goddamnit!

WILDCAT: *(He is stunned. He waits before speaking.)*
Was she married before? Seems like everyone's been
married before.

FRANK: Divorced, no kids.

WILDCAT: So your first wife is dead. What happened
with the second one?

FRANK: Lynn, the first one, died after the divorce. I
guess you could say we just grew apart. I don't know
what the hell the second marriage was about. Four
months and we hated each other.

WILDCAT: *(Shakes his head and takes a drink)* I wouldn't
know where to find a woman today. I mean if I was in
the market.

FRANK: You didn't say if you have kids.

WILDCAT: I got some, and grandkids, too. I never see
them, though. They all think I'm crazy as hell. Well,
screw them, too. I guess you have grandkids?

FRANK: Rob and his wife Cindy have two girls. They're
out back. Don't say a word when I tell you their names.
Mellow and Peace.

WILDCAT: *(Drops his jaw to exaggerate his disbelief.)*
Mellow and Peace? Those are hippie names.

FRANK: They're good kids, actually. Rob and Cindy
are good parents. *(Laughs lightly)* I think Cindy named
them. She grew up California.

WILDCAT: Those goddamn hippies. I still get pissed
when I think of them calling us baby killers. For years
I didn't dare tell anyone I'd been to Nam. *(Points to his
baseball cap)* Now I tell every son-of-a-bitch I can that I
was over there and I don't give a good rat's ass what
they think. Heh, you still smoke weed?

FRANK: Not since Nam.

WILDCAT: I still do it a little bit.

FRANK: (*Smiles as he remembers*) I'd never tried it until Joker talked me into it. We were on L Z Maple. After that, we got high every time we came out of the field. He never told me where he got it.

WILDCAT: Joker's the one who got me started on it, too.

FRANK: I lost my appetite for it after what happened at Tri Binh. (*Pauses with a smile*) He'd get me laughing so hard I'd pee in my pants. (*Pauses again, tries to speak, then shakes his head*) I couldn't have had a better buddy. (*He suddenly and angrily slams a fist on the recliner's armrest and jumps up.*) Yeah, Joker was dead, all right, when I carried him to the dustoff. Goddamnit, I never should have let Betty do this! And now you tell me fucking Brooks is coming here, coming into my own house!

WILDCAT: (*Gently sets his beer onto the coffee table. He studies* FRANK, *looks around the room, looks over his shoulder. Finally, he speaks.*) Sorry, Frank. Hell, we don't have to talk about anything. I'm just glad to see an old buddy. I just wish Joker could be here.

(*Blackout*)

(*End of scene*)

Scene 2

(*The* WEST *living room about thirty minutes later*)

(*At rise:* FRANK *is alone and sitting in the same recliner. He is lost in thought and staring straight ahead, just as he was at the beginning of Scene 1.*)

(BETTY, ROB *and* CINDY *enter from stage right. Each carries a beer. All three are animated from the effects of alcohol.*)

BETTY: Hi, soldier. (*Wiggles her hips, smiling flirtatiously.*) Looking for a good time?

(ROB *and* CINDY *laugh in unison.*)

FRANK: *(Continues staring ahead, emotionless)* Let me know if you need any help with anything.

ROB: It's all taken care of, Dad. I just flipped the steaks again. We just wanted to see how you and Wildcat were doing.

(ROB *Looks around the room.*) Heh, where'd he go?

BETTY: Yeah, where's your buddy, Cherryboy?

FRANK: In the guest room. He said he needed a nap.

CINDY: The girls are whipping up the cole slaw and potato salad. You can eat right after your other friend gets here.

ROB: *(Laughs)* I told Cindy and Betty how Bangkok Billy got his name. That's a classic. When's he supposed to get here?

FRANK: No idea.

BETTY: *(Drinking from her beer, she starts to lean sideways as though to fall and grabs onto* ROB.*)* Oh, it won't be long, I'm sure.

FRANK: *(Still staring ahead)* He's bringing someone. Alphonso told me.

CINDY: *(Enthusiastically)* His wife? Great. We've got enough steaks for a—what do you call it? —a squadron.

ROB: *(Laughs again as he affectionately drapes his arm around* CINDY's *shoulder.*) Hell, even I know it's the Air Force that has squadrons. She means squad, right, Dad?

FRANK: A guy named Joey Brooks is driving him. I used to know him.

ROB: Another buddy? What did you guys call him?

FRANK: *(Unconvincingly)* I forget.

BETTY: Well, I don't care if you called him Howdy Doody. Any man who helped protect this great country of ours is welcome here anytime.

CINDY: I second the motion.

ROB: *(Steps close to* FRANK *and fondly pats his shoulder.)* This is going to be great, Dad. Four of you.

CINDY: We better go check on the girls. Sometimes I don't think they even know how to pour a bowl of cereal.

*(*CINDY *exits right with* ROB *following.)*

BETTY: *(Moves behind* FRANK, *places her beer on the end table beside his recliner, and begins squeezing and massaging his shoulders.)* I would have been a sophomore in good old Pioneer High when you were in Vietnam. *(Shakes her head.)* There was so much going on back then. There was a boy on our street, Willie something. He went to Vietnam, but I think he was in the Navy. I don't think I knew any others.

*(*FRANK *closes his eyes and tries to relax while* BETTY *massages him:)*

FRANK: They ended the draft about the time you graduated, that's why.

BETTY: I can't imagine what that was like. You graduate from high school one day, and get drafted the next.

FRANK: I was stupid to go in at all. We were all stupid.

BETTY: *(Pauses her massage, leans over* FRANK's *shoulder and looks him in the face.)* Stupid? No. You did what you were supposed to do.

FRANK: I should have run off to Canada.

BETTY: *(Mildly shocked, she quickly steps around the recliner to face* FRANK.) How can you say that?

FRANK: *(Stands, walks to the room's front window and stares outside.)* It was all for nothing. How many thousands of names are on that wall? I want you to give me just one of those names, Betty. *(Turns toward BETTY.)* Can you do that for me? Just one name?

BETTY: *(Her face is awash with hurt. She tries several times before managing to speak.)* You know I can't. *(She is close to crying.)* This is so wrong, Frank. You and Wildcat and Billy and whoever he's bringing put your lives on the line for your country. What's wrong with having a special day for you and your buddies? Please, Frank. Oh, God, please don't ruin everything.

FRANK: *(He slowly nods in agreement)* I'll be good. Promise.

(The doorbell rings. BETTY looks at FRANK who hesitates before gesturing for her to answer the door. She slowly approaches the door while he steps backward. BETTY takes a deep breath and exhales before opening the door. Two men enter, one behind the other. The first is BANGKOK BILLY HUSTAD, and he is only a couple inches taller than Betty. He is leaning forward awkwardly on two canes. He wears an olive drab t-shirt across which is emblazoned in red "SOUTHEAST ASIAN WAR GAMES, SECOND PLACE." The t-shirt almost covers his ample gut. He wears jeans with sandals attached to his prostheses. He is stooped, and sprouts a gray pony tail that extends half-way down his back. The second man is JOEY "HARDROCK" BROOKS who towers behind BILLY. He is slim and muscular. His thick, gray hair is parted and neatly brushed. He wears a white sports shirt and casual slacks. Both men are smiling broadly.)

BILLY: I'm Billy Hustad, Mama San! *(Canes in hand, he throws open his arms and tightly hugs BETTY. He rocks her back and forth before letting her go.)* You number one mama san. I can tell.

BETTY: *(Smiling but taken aback.)* So good to finally meet you, Billy! *(She looks over his shoulder to* JOEY.*)* And you, too. Frank told me your name, but I'm sorry I forgot.

*(*JOEY *grins, steps inside, and extends his hand, which* BETTY *shakes.)*

JOEY: Joey Brooks.

BETTY: *(Steps aside and sweeps an open arm toward* FRANK.*)* Well, guys. There's your man.

*(*BILLY *and* JOEY *stare at* FRANK *and slowly break into grins.* FRANK *gradually returns the grins.)*

BILLY: Cherryboy, you son-of-a-bitch!

(Completely dependent on his canes, BILLY *hobbles stiffly to* FRANK *and smothers him with a hug. His canes drop to the floor.* FRANK*, at a loss, slowly wraps his arms around* BILLY's *lower back.* FRANK *momentarily relaxes his grip, but* BILLY *grunts as he hugs harder for another ten or fifteen seconds before pulling himself away but leaving his arms on* FRANK's *shoulders for balance. There are tears on his cheeks:)*

BILLY: Love, ya, man. Love, ya.

*(*JOEY *leans over, picks up* BILLY's *canes, and hands them to* BILLY. *He extends a hand to* FRANK, *and* FRANK *pointedly hesitates before taking it:)*

JOEY: Good to see you, Frank.

FRANK: Yeah, you, too. *(He gestures an open hand toward* BETTY.*)* Guys, this is Betty. She organized the whole thing.

BILLY: So you're the fox who took Frank's cherry.

FRANK: *(Amused)* She wasn't the first, Billy, but that's another story. I've been very lucky.

BILLY: More than me, that's for sure.

JOEY: We can't thank you enough for putting this together, ma'am.

BILLY: *(Nodding toward* JOEY*)* Call him Hardrock, ma'am.

JOEY: *(Laughing lightly.)* Never mind him, Betty. Hardrock was a long time ago.

BETTY: *(Hands on hips, her eyes sweep all three. She nods her head approvingly.)* This is absolutely amazing.

WILDCAT: *(Suddenly enters from stage right. He is wearing his hat.)* I'd know those voices anywhere! Second squad, the meanest bastards in the valley of death!

BILLY: *(Laughing enthusiastically)* Wildcat, you old son-of-bitch! Last time I saw you you was carrying me to that dustoff.

*(*BILLY *opens his arms as* WILDCAT *quickly steps into them. They hug and rock, and repeatedly pat each other's backs.* BILLY*'s canes fall to the floor again, and* JOEY *picks them up and holds them.* WILDCAT *lets go of* BILLY *and throws his arms around* JOEY*. Meanwhile,* BILLY *grabs* WILDCAT*'s shoulder to stabilize himself. Finally, smiling ecstatically,* WILDCAT *steps back from* JOEY *and examines him from head to toe.)*

WILDCAT: *(Laughing)* How come you ain't dead, man? I heard in the hospital they weren't able to save you. Damn, it's good to see you.

JOEY: *(Smiles reservedly)* I heard the same about you, Wildcat.

WILDCAT: You know what I remember about you? You sure know how to tie a tourniquet. Jesus, I'd have been drained dry before the dustoff got there if it hadn't been for you, and I wouldn't have been able to carry Billy. And there you were all ripped apart yourself.

BETTY: *(She has been listening in astonishment)* Gentlemen—

BILLY: Attention! Female in the barracks!

(WILDCAT and BILLY, still supporting himself on WILDCAT's shoulder, laugh and awkwardly snap to attention. JOEY laughs to himself while FRANK shakes his head in amusement.)

BETTY: I was just going to say that we've got all the beer you want, and the steaks and everything else are as good as done. The house is yours. We're all just going to leave you alone to enjoy yourselves until we're ready to eat. *(She spontaneously approaches FRANK and kisses him.)* I love you, Frank West, and all your buddies. *(Exits right.)*

BILLY: *(Taking his canes from JOEY)* Jesus, what a woman.

FRANK: Sit down, you guys.

(FRANK returns to his recliner. BILLY joins WILDCAT on the sofa, and JOEY takes the vacant recliner. MELLOW and PEACE enter from stage right. Each carries two beers. They pause in the center of the room, uncertain what to do, then approach FRANK.)

MELLOW: *(Extending a beer toward FRANK)* Grandma said to give this to you. She said it's okay this time.

BILLY: *(Laughing)* Watch it, Cherryboy. The gooks might have booby trapped that beer can.

FRANK: *(Ignoring BILLY, and proudly addressing his guests.)* These two beautiful ladies belong to my son. *(He hesitates before taking the beer from MELLOW, then motions for the girls to distribute the others.)*

WILDCAT: *(Laughing while taking the other beer from MELLOW.)* Tell Billy and Joey the girls' names, Frank.

FRANK: *(Pointing to each girl as he introduces them.)* Mellow and Peace. You'll meet my son and his wife later.

BILLY: Mellow? Like when you get stoned?

WILDCAT: I think those are beautiful names.

FRANK: Thanks, girls.

(MELLOW and PEACE exit right, WILDCAT gazing lustfully at them as they disappear.)

JOEY: You're very fortunate, Frank. Grandkids kind of close the circle.

WILDCAT: You're a grandpa, too? Hell, you don't look it.

BILLY: *(Somberly)* He won't tell you, Wildcat. Hardrock's grandson got the shit shot out of him in Afghanistan last year.

WILDCAT: Oh, God. I'm so sorry, Hardrock. Afghanistan. Goddamnit, we better win that one.

JOEY: He'll be okay, but thanks. And I've got a couple beautiful granddaughters. You?

WILDCAT: Oh, yeah. Four, five, six. *(Drinks from his beer.)* Hell, if I know how many.

BILLY: *(Slipping down into the sofa)* Kids. Well, that's a bullet I dodged. Ain't no broad yet ever told me I knocked her up.

WILDCAT: *(Hoisting his beer toward BILLY)* Man, if you can get women without having any legs, here's to you. I don't think I'd ever have the guts to leave my house.

BILLY: Hell, I can get a woman anytime I want. You wouldn't believe how easy it is.

(The four men drink their beers until BILLY speaks.)

BILLY: Old Joker. Now he would have been a great grandpa.

WILDCAT: I was telling Frank before you guys got here how that guy could make a joke out of anything. *(Laughing.)* I burned a leech off his ass one time and he asked me if I also did massages.

BILLY: *(Shaking his head in disgust)* Goddamn leeches. I was always finding those ugly bloodsuckers in my crotch. They swelled up as big as cigars sometimes.

WILDCAT: *(Also shaking his head)* And those big red ants that fell like nuts out of the trees.

BILLY: And the rain. I tell people I used to sleep sitting up in mud but they don't believe me. Heh, Frank, you and Joker were buddies, right?

(FRANK glances quickly at JOEY, shifts uncomfortably in his recliner, and nods slightly. JOEY looks away from FRANK.)

BILLY: I still remember him talking about how he was going to go to Australia for R and R and become a cowboy. *(Laughs)* Crazy guy. He was going to be a sheep rancher.

FRANK: *(Realizing the others are waiting for him to respond.)* He wanted to go check it out was all.

WILDCAT: R and R. Hell, I never got mine. You got yours, right, Joey?

JOEY: *(Smiling)* Taiwan. Five days and nights of drinking and screwing.

WILDCAT: Damn! Where'd you go, Frank?

(FRANK slowly sips his beer, trying to formulate a response.)

BILLY: I remember this now, Cherryboy. Joker told me. You and him was going to go to Australia together.

FRANK: That was the plan.

BILLY: Yeah, you guys were all set to go in a couple days, but then we went into that ville and that madman Stokely went crazy with the artillery. What was the name of that ville?

WILDCAT: Tri Binh. Frank and I were talking about it this morning.

BILLY: Somebody should have fragged that bastard lieutenant the day he got in-country. Dumb prick couldn't even read a map.

WILDCAT: You know, that day is still a complete dream to me. I remember we got snipper fire, and I remember the lieutenant sending our squad into the ville. I remember you, Joey, using your shirt to make a tourniquet for me, and I remember somehow carrying Billy to the dustoff. And I remember Cherryboy carrying poor Joker to the dustoff. After that, I get lost. I mean, I have no memory of the artillery. Maybe I got knocked out.

BILLY: You don't remember the lieutenant screaming we were getting overrun?

WILDCAT: Not really.

BILLY: That's when he went psycho and called in the artillery. I remember you and Joey bleeding all over the place.

WILDCAT: I hope they gave you a hundred percent, Joey.

JOEY: (Contentedly) Seventy. Lost some muscle here and there. Lost some hearing like you guys probably did. It wasn't that bad.

WILDCAT: Just seventy? Goddamn V A.

JOEY: No, seventy was about right in my case.

WILDCAT: (Visibly upset) How can you say that? You didn't appeal?

JOEY: *(Laughing lightly)* No. I worked at V A for twenty-seven years. I processed a lot of claims. Seventy percent was fair in my case.

WILDCAT: What? I hate the V A. Every Vietnam vet I know hates the V A.

BILLY: Tell him what you told me driving up here, Joey.

(JOEY takes a long drink, leans forward and sets the empty can on the floor. WILDCAT leans forward, mouth open. FRANK takes a drink and readjusts himself in his recliner.)

JOEY: *(Takes a deep breath and exhales)* After I got out of the hospital at Fort Lewis, I came home to Tulsa and tried junior college. I just couldn't focus on it. And the girls there, hell, once they found out I'd been to Nam they wouldn't have a thing to do with me. So I tried a lot of stuff like you guys probably did. I gave college another try several years later and I did okay. Met my wife, and everything. I actually became a grade school teacher, but I really didn't know what I wanted to do. Meanwhile, I'd stayed friends with this vet I'd met in a psychology class. He'd lost both legs like Billy but both were A K. One night he rolled his wheelchair on purpose right out in front of a bus and that was that. I never cried in Nam, but I cried about that. *(Shrugs)* It was like finding God or something. I cried but I got pissed, too. I went down to V A and filled out an application. They took me. I guess I just thought I needed to do what I could for guys like us. Hell, nobody else would.

WILDCAT: *(Shaking his head)* I guess some guys at the V A weren't so bad.

JOEY: I dealt everyday with angry vets, really, really angry vets. But there's something more. *(Stands nervously and turns to BILLY.)* And I didn't tell you this in the car, Billy, and I've never even told my wife this. *(Struggling not to cry)* We did a lot of bad shit in

Nam, at least I know I did. Working for V A, well, it
just felt like when I was helping guys get themselves
back together I was also helping put Vietnam back
together, especially those kids in those villages. *(Crying
momentarily, he wipes his eyes with his shirt and looks at the
floor.)* I don't know how to put it.

WILDCAT: *(Removes his cap, wipes his eyes with it, and
drops it in his lap.)* You're beautiful, man. Never thought
I'd see old Hardrock get weepy eyed.

(There is a prolonged silence until FRANK speaks.)

FRANK: Goddamnit. We haven't seen each other in
more than fifty years. What the hell are we doing
talking about Nam?

BILLY: *(Testily)* Man, Nam is all we've got. *(Finishes his
beer in one guzzle, and drops the empty can on the coffee
table.)*

FRANK: Well, maybe it's all you've got.

JOEY: Frank's right, Billy. Hell, everybody's had a
Vietnam of some sort and they still talk about other
things. Anybody following the Royals this year? My
wife and I are their biggest fans.

BILLY: *(Bitterly)* Who gives a rat's ass? You need two
legs to play baseball.

*(MELLOW and PEACE enter from stage right with another
round of beers. The men stop speaking, take the beers, and
nod their thanks to the girls. They are silent until the girls
have disappeared at stage right.)*

WILDCAT: *(Sips his beer)* We need to mellow out. Hell,
we're alive. Ain't nobody shooting at us now. God has
a purpose for all of us, I'm just telling you.

BILLY: *(Increasingly bitter)* Oh, really? What kind of
god—

WILDCAT: That's enough, Billy! All I know is if you don't believe in God you're fucked.

JOEY: *(Interrupting)* My wife and I drove to the Grand Canyon this summer. Any of you guys ever been there? The pictures don't do it justice. Frank?

FRANK: *(Shrugs)* Never really had the urge to travel after Nam.

WILDCAT: I have a friend in the Legion. We like to go to San Padre Island.

BILLY: *(Still angry as he struggles to raise himself in the sofa.)* You mean the American Legion?

WILDCAT: *(Defensively)* What's wrong with the Legion? I have lots of friends in the Legion.

BILLY: Just a bunch of old drunks who never saw combat, always talking like John Wayne on Iwo Jima. Don't tell me you wear one of those stupid caps.

WILDCAT: *(Jumping up and leaning over BILLY)* I ought to rip that damn shirt off your back right now! It's insulting as hell!

JOEY: *(Standing and raising his hands as though to halt traffic.)* Save it, guys. We're just here for a barbecue and good times. What would Joker think of us acting like this? *(He waits, then slowly sits.)*

WILDCAT: *(Returns to his place on the sofa, and drinks from his beer.)* Speaking of Joker, I still don't understand what happened at Tri Binh. Lieutenant Stokely really went crazy?

BILLY: Sure as hell did.

WILDCAT: *(Shakes his head)* So he called in arty right on top of us?

BILLY: Right on top of us but it mostly came down on him and Joker. Frank and Joey were right under it, too.

The rest of second squad was squatting behind a bunch of banana trees. I can still see it.

WILDCAT: I was telling Frank when I got here I remember him all bloody and carrying Joker over his shoulder to the dustoff. I remember thinking Joker was already K I A.

BILLY: You and Joker probably would have loved Australia, Cherryboy. I heard they had some pretty good round-eye stuff down there, but not as good as that slant-eye pussy in Bangkok.

FRANK: *(Agitated)* I need to say this for Joker. You don't know what you're talking about, Billy. He never said anything about going there just to get laid for five days and nights. All he wanted was to go check it out for this ranch he was thinking about. He got me stoned and convinced me to go with him.

WILDCAT: Why Australia? You could have a ranch in Wyoming.

FRANK: *(Takes a long swallow of beer. Visibly angry, his voice rises.)* How dumb can the three of you be? Isn't it obvious? *(Looks at each man separately before resuming)* I didn't want to get into this but you're really pissing me off. We were going to go there and never come back. Got it?

WILDCAT: *(Disbelieving)* Go AWOL? You mean desert your own squad? Us?

FRANK: *(He chugs the remainder of his beer.)* Bingo! We were all set, had our tickets and everything. And then goddamn Tri Binh. We were supposed to leave in two goddamn days! You never would have seen us again. *(Throws his empty beer can across the room.)*

(WILDCAT slowly adjusts his cap. BILLY slips further into the sofa. JOEY looks at Frank, then stares away. There is a lengthy silence while the men concentrate on their beers.)

WILDCAT: Wow. You were really going to do that to us?

BILLY: It's okay, man. Making me come back to Nam from R and R was the cruelest thing the Army did to me. All I came back for was to get my goddamn legs blown off.

(There is another prolonged silence.)

BILLY: I'll tell you what, guys. If Joker was here he'd step outside right now and toke a joint. *(Pats his pants pocket, looks around the room, and uses his canes to stand.)* Anyone want to join me?

WILDCAT: Do what you have to do, Billy. I'm okay with beer for now.

BILLY: Suit yourself. *(He labors for the front door, opens it, steps outside, and closes it behind him.)*

WILDCAT: He was stoned the whole time we were over there.

JOEY: *(Shakes his head)* He smoked a joint on the drive up here. I didn't say anything for a long time. I just kept my window open. I had no idea he's in such bad shape.

WILDCAT: Sad. Really, really sad. Can't you guys at V A do something for him?

JOEY: Not unless he wants the help. *(Shakes his head again.)* I used to see guys like Billy all the time.

WILDCAT: You think he might kill himself someday?

JOEY: *(Takes a deep breath and exhales)* I hope not. Some do, some don't. Some even kill their wives or bosses first.

FRANK: How the hell can you assholes talk like that? He's one of us, for Christ's sake!

JOEY: *(Calmly raises a an open hand toward* FRANK.*)* Sorry. All I meant was Billy is headed for real trouble unless he wants to help the people who would be willing to help him. I went on and on about this with him while we were in the car. He finally told me to screw myself and mind my own business. We didn't talk the last hour of the drive.

WILDCAT: *(Agitated, he stands)* Know what? I'm going to join Billy outside. He needs us.

FRANK: He doesn't need it that way.

WILDCAT: We all imbibed over there, Cherryboy. You told me you and Joker did it all the time.

FRANK: And I told you I lost all taste for the stuff the day Joker died.

WILDCAT: You smoked, too, didn't you, Joey?

JOEY: Not a lot.

WILDCAT: Well, there you go. I'll be with Billy.

(Exits through the front door.)

JOEY: *(Finishes his beer and sets the can on the coffee table)* Honestly, Frank, I'm not trying to ruin the day.

FRANK: Ah, forget it.

JOEY: From the looks of things you've done well. I'm proud of you.

FRANK: You don't know me well enough to say you're proud of me, especially after what you did at Tri Binh. You haven't seen me since that day so screw you.

JOEY: *(Shakes his head)* The last thing I want to do is piss you off.

FRANK: You're doing a good job of it.

JOEY: *(Thinks for a moment)* When Billy found me on Facebook I was overjoyed. The first thing that came to my mind was he's alive. One-third of us Viet vets are gone already, if you can believe that. I wrote back and told him we needed to get together. And then he told me he'd linked up with you and Wildcat. Believe it or not, that was the happiest day I'd had in a long time.

(ROB *and* CINDY, *hand-in-hand but with beers in their free hands, enter from stage right, laughing loudly and excessively.*)

ROB: Gentlemen, Sergeant Betty West says you need to start moving to the backyard. Everything's ready. Heh, where's Billy and Wildcat? We want to meet Billy and Wildcat.

CINDY: *(Sniffs repeatedly, then smiles.)* I recognize that fine, sweet aroma. California grown, no doubt. I bet they stepped outside.

(CINDY *extends a beer to* FRANK *who quickly grabs it.*)

FRANK: *(Sarcastically)* They're bonding.

(ROB *laughs, hands* JOEY *a beer:*)

ROB: I hope they don't bond too much. There aren't enough steaks for thirds, if you know what I mean.

CINDY: *(Also laughs)* I bet you guys bonded like that a lot in Vietnam.

FRANK: *(Ignoring* CINDY*)* We'll join everybody as soon as we can.

ROB: No pressure, Dad. No pressure.

(ROB *and* CINDY, *still holding hands, exit right laughing.*)

FRANK: *(Suddenly aggressive)* Why exactly did you come here, Brooks?

JOEY: Billy invited me to tag along.

FRANK: That's not what I meant.

JOEY: I know.

FRANK: Didn't it cross your mind I wouldn't want to see you? You could have said no.

JOEY: I thought long and hard about it. I just needed to see you, even if you hate me for what I did to Joker.

FRANK: Are you looking for some sort of forgiveness? You won't get it from me, that's for sure.

JOEY: I think about Tri Binh and Joker everyday, Frank. I came to the conclusion years ago that I didn't do anything that requires forgiveness. I just want peace. I thought talking to you like this would help.

FRANK: Well, you need to keep thinking about it. I hope Joker haunts you forever.

JOEY: *(Nods resignedly)* I'm sure he will.

(The voices of BILLY *and* WILDCAT *are audible from stage left. They enter through the front door laughing uncontrollably.* BILLY *wobbles on his canes as he heads toward the sofa.* WILDCAT *wraps an arm around his shoulder to keep him from falling.)*

BILLY: *(Stopping and turning toward* FRANK *and* JOEY*)* You guys know what? I feel like I'm on my last leg. *(Laughs hard enough to begin coughing.)*

WILDCAT: *(His arm still around* BILLY*, laughs with him)* Good one, Billy. That's a good one.

FRANK: *(Stands)* Everything's ready. *(Nods toward stage right)* That way. There's a couple steps down into the back yard, Billy, but first I want to say something to all of you. No more talk about Nam, and no more talk about Joker. Got it?

BILLY: *(Still laughing)* Roger that, Cherryboy. Wildcat and me will take point.

WILDCAT: Damn straight. And we'll shoot anything that moves.

(BILLY *and* WILDCAT *slowly move toward stage right and continue laughing.)*

JOEY: Easy, Billy. Hold onto him, Wildcat.

WILDCAT: That's affirmative, Hardrock.

BILLY: And no chowing down until we've set out the Claymores!

WILDCAT: It's second squad against the world, by God.

(BILLY *and* WILDCAT *exit right.* FRANK *and* JOEY *remain behind.)*

FRANK: They have no idea what really happened at Tri Binh, do they?

JOEY: Just you and me.

FRANK: *(Speaking with a strong hint of a threat)* Just be sure you keep it that way.

(FRANK *exits stage right.* JOEY *hesitates before following.)*

(Blackout)

(End of scene)

END OF ACT ONE

ACT TWO

Scene 1

(The WEST *living room three hours later)*

(At rise: The room's window shades remain up, but it is dark outside. The floor lamps and the lamp on the end table beside FRANK's *recliner are on.* BILLY *is sleeping on his back on the sofa. His two canes are strategically placed beside each other on the floor and parallel to the sofa. There are five beer cans on the coffee table.)*

*(*WILDCAT, JOEY *and* FRANK *enter from stage right.* WILDCAT *and* FRANK *carry beers.* FRANK *returns to his recliner.)*

WILDCAT: *(Stopping in mid-step as he looks at* BILLY*)* Damn. He hasn't moved a bit, poor guy. How come your toenails grow back but not your legs?

JOEY: *(Dropping into the other recliner)* Ah, just let him sleep.

WILDCAT: You think it's true what he was crying about just before he passed out?

JOEY: Just let it go, Wildcat.

WILDCAT: He looks so small. *(He squeezes onto the sofa near* BILLY's *head.)* I shouldn't have smoked that weed. I thought the beers would mellow me out.

JOEY: Okay if we leave Wildcat's car here tonight, Frank? I can drive us all to the motel.

FRANK: *(Irritably)* Fine.

WILDCAT: Hell, just give me another hour or so and I can drive.

FRANK: Joey's going to drive, Wildcat, so go ahead and drink yourself to death. Screw it.

JOEY: You've got a great family, Frank. They love the hell out of you.

FRANK: Sometimes, maybe.

WILDCAT: Tonight they sure as hell did. If I was Peace's age again I'd be dating her. You know, I wonder about my grandkids sometimes. The one's I know about, I mean. Some days I can't even remember their names.

JOEY: I don't want to get too much into it, Wildcat, but I worked with lots of guys like you at the V A. You need to reach out to your kids, your grandkids. I'm telling you, family makes all the difference.

WILDCAT: *(Shakes his head.)* They could all be on Mars for all I know. *(Lifts his beer, then quickly lowers it.)* I bet Joker would have had a hundred kids. He ever say anything to you about having kids, Frank?

JOEY: I thought we agreed with Frank not to talk about Nam anymore.

FRANK: Ah, screw it. He used to say once we got our sheep ranch started we'd hire those Australian cowgirls. Kids probably would have followed.

WILDCAT: Lots of them, if I knew Joker.

FRANK: *(Encouraged, he takes a long drink.)* He was serious. Sometimes at night on L Z Osage we'd sit on top of our bunker and get stoned out of our minds. He'd lay it out over and over, about how we were going to take off for the Outback as soon as we landed in Sydney. 'They'll never find us,' he'd say.

WILDCAT: *(Laughing)* You guys got stoned on perimeter duty? Holy shit!

FRANK: Yep. We just didn't care. You remember how it was, Wildcat. We figured we were going to get killed anyway, so why not get killed while you're stoned.

WILDCAT: How the hell did you guys think you'd get the money for a ranch?

FRANK: *(Shrugs)* He said we'd get jobs when it was safe and save up for it. Then he'd find the cowgirls. No cowboys, just cowgirls.

WILDCAT: Just like that?

FRANK: Just like that.

WILDCAT: And never come back to the States?

FRANK: *(He pauses, then sweeps the room with his free arm.)* And never come back to the States, never come back to any of this bullshit!

JOEY: Relax, Frank. It's okay.

FRANK: *(His voice rises as his anger grows. He speaks while staring at the ceiling.)* I told Betty not to have this reunion or whatever the hell it is. I hate even thinking about Nam, but, since you bastards want to hear about it so much here it is. You can have your goddamn American Legion, Wildcat. Go to your stupid meetings and recite your silly Pledge of Allegiance and all that stuff. Joker made me see the light. Remember when Boomer Bass blew away that little girl about a week before Tri Binh? She was laughing and running up to him like she thought Boomer was going to give her a piece of candy like we sometimes did. He emptied an entire magazine into her, said he thought she was carrying a booby trap. He just wanted the thrill of killing a gook, even a little girl. Everybody saw him do it, but Lieutenant Stokley just acted like nothing happened. Joker and I promised ourselves that night

that we were done with America, kids like us getting
drafted by the thousands who didn't know a damn
thing, and sending us off to rice paddies to die for
nothing and to kill little girls for nothing. I've seen it
over and over again. Kids like Joey's grandson, getting
fucked up or killed in Somalia, Iraq, Afghanistan and
God knows where. We have to protect America, they
say, this place where our marriages go to hell, where
we have to live with people we hate, and get fired from
lousy jobs we hate, and then get old and die without a
dime to our name. *(Quickly turns toward* JOEY *and yells)*
You ruined my life that day!

WILDCAT: *(Rising suddenly)* Hold on, Cherryboy! You're
way out of line. Joey didn't do anything to you.

FRANK: *(Staring hard at* JOEY*)* The hell he didn't!

BILLY: *(Squirms and groans as he awakens and tries to prop
himself up.)* What the hell's all the shouting?

WILDCAT: *(Settles back onto the sofa, and strokes* BILLY's
hair.) You okay, buddy?

BILLY: *(Looks around the room, then at* WILDCAT, FRANK,
and JOEY*.)* How the hell did I get here? Jesus, I'm
messed up.

WILDCAT: Just a few too many beers.

BILLY: *(Struggles until he is erect)* I need a hit, man.

JOEY: Go back to sleep, Billy.

WILDCAT: You want a sandwich or something? Maybe
a glass of milk? That's what I always do. You didn't eat
that much.

BILLY: Naw. Water maybe.

WILDCAT: You got it, Billy. *(Stands laughing)* And I
won't put no iodine tablets in it. *(Exits right.)*

BILLY: *(Laughs lightly and shakes his head)* I forgot all
about those damn iodine tablets. I can't believe how

we had to fill our canteens with village well water sometimes. I think the gooks must have pissed in their own wells. Animals. I can still taste iodine sometimes.

JOEY: Just relax, Billy. We don't have to leave until you're up for it.

BILLY: *(Looks sheepishly at* FRANK*)* I kind of remember your wife giving me a steak. I bet I made an ass of myself.

FRANK: You just drank a little too much. I'm sure Betty and everyone else understood.

*(*WILDCAT *enters from stage right and hands* BILLY *a glass of water. He also carries a beer for himself:)*

WILDCAT: One-hundred percent pure water, Billy. No iodine. *(He sits again beside* BILLY.*)*

BILLY: *(Eyes* FRANK *suspiciously)* I didn't say anything about, well, weird stuff when we were eating, did I? About me, I mean?

WILDCAT: *(Sitting)* It's okay, Billy. It's nobody's damn business anyway.

BILLY: *(Twists angrily toward* WILDCAT*)* I blabbered away like a drunken fool, didn't I? I probably cried, too.

FRANK: I just told him he didn't say anything stupid, Wildcat. What the hell are you doing?

BILLY: *(Impulsively throws his water glass across the room.)* Screw you guys! *(Begins crying openly.)*

JOEY: *(Stands, walks to* BILLY, *and leans over him. He tries to put his arm on his shoulder but* BILLY *slaps it away.)* It's nothing to be ashamed of, Billy.

BILLY: *(Crying while the others look on uncertainly. He wipes his eyes with his shirt sleeve.)* They told me when I woke up from surgery in Nam that my legs were history. But I knew it was worse than that. They had me on a catheter so I could pee okay, but it still hurt like hell down there. I was afraid to look. The bastards waited three whole days before telling me one of my balls was gone.

WILDCAT: Let it go, Billy.

BILLY: Let it go? Ha! Then they sent me to Japan to chop me up even more, and then to Walter Reed for a whole year. I tried everything I could to get it up. *(Briefly resumes crying)* I haven't been laid since R and R in Bangkok! What kind of man does that make me? There's no point in living if you can't get laid!

JOEY: They should have told you it doesn't matter if you've only got one. I know for a fact—

BILLY: They told me a hundred times! Twice, right after I got out of the Army, I got a woman in a bar so drunk she took pity on me and took me home. No legs and one ball. Those women tried everything but it didn't work. One of them even punched me out so I hit her back with my cane. She called the cops and guess who spent the night in jail? Can you believe that crap?

JOEY: I keep telling you to let me set you up with V A, Billy. They've got people who...

BILLY: Screw the goddamn V A! You think I haven't tried that? Jesus! *(He looks at the others one-at-a-time.)* I never should have come to this goddamn party.

JOEY: *(Again tries putting his arm on BILLY who this time doesn't resist.)* Well, I for one think we really did need to see each other again. We should have done it a long time ago if we'd known how to find each other.

BILLY: I should have gone AWOL in Bangkok just like Frank and Joker were going to do in Australia. You better believe I thought about it. *(Chuckles)* One day I got laid four times with four different women. I was stoned the whole time. Man, that was the happiest I've

ever been in my life. And then Tri Binh. You know
what? We'd be better off if we'd all been killed!

WILDCAT: That's bullshit! Yeah, it's been tough but I've
still been able to do things. You can, too.

BILLY: Like what? Tell us, Wildcat. Tell us all the
amazing things you've done with your life since Nam.
Did you become a doctor? Are you rich? Did you
become an airline pilot? Tell us!

WILDCAT: I just mean I've done okay. You know,
worked and had kids and stuff.

BILLY: Hell, you're just like me. If you weren't getting
money every month from Uncle Sam you'd be out on
the streets.

WILDCAT: Speak for yourself! (*Chugs his beer, and
emphatically sets the empty can on the floor.*) I'm driving
my own car tonight, and not to any motel with you
guys. I'm going home. No offense, Frank, but this little
party has been a bust.

FRANK: No argument from me.

(ROB *and* CINDY *enter from stage right. Their balance is
uncertain as they negotiate their way to where they can face*
FRANK *and his guests.* MELLOW *and* PEACE *follow.*)

ROB: Cindy and I need to be going—

CINDY: (*Laughing*) Before we're too messed up.

ROB: But we just want to say what an honor—

CINDY: (*Clasping her hands and bowing*) We're so proud
of you guys. We owe all our freedoms to you. (*Turns to
her daughters.*) Girls, you need to thank these brave men
for all the sacrifices they've made for you.

(CINDY *steps aside and motions for* MELLOW *and* PEACE
*to say something. They awkwardly mumble various
gratitudes.*)

ROB: We just want to say what an honor this has been. None of the guys I work with were ever in the military—

CINDY: And It's a shame, a real shame.

ROB: But this has been a real opportunity for us to learn something about our great country and the men who have kept it that way. I just wish you'd tell us how you got hurt.

WILDCAT: *(Standing uncertainly)* Just doing our jobs, sir. Sir and ma'am.

JOEY: *(Still standing near* BILLY*)* You're both very kind. You've got a great dad, Rob.

ROB: *(Turns his attention to* FRANK. *He chokes up while trying to speak.)* He...he's the greatest. He...

CINDY: *(Slips her arm around* ROB's *waist)* Absolutely the greatest. You're all the greatest.

ROB: He...I can't imagine doing what you guys did at such a young age. Hell, you weren't much older than our girls. *(Moves toward* FRANK *and opens his arms.)* Dad...

(Caught off guard, FRANK *stands and allows* ROB *to embrace him.* FRANK *slowly returns the embrace. While he does so,* CINDY *unabashedly hugs* WILDCAT, *then* JOEY. *She moves toward the sofa where* BILLY *remains sitting.)*

CINDY: *(Leaning forward and hugging* BILLY*)* We love you, Billy. Everyone loves you. You don't need to feel ashamed about anything. There's a special woman out there somewhere for you, a very special woman.

BILLY: *(Without conviction)* Sure.

*(*ROB *and his family move toward the front door.* ROB *holds it open while* CINDY *and their daughters exit.)*

ROB: I volunteered to help clean up, Dad, but Betty wouldn't have it.

FRANK: Don't worry about it, son.

ROB: And don't worry about us. Mellow's going to drive.

(ROB shuts the door behind him, and FRANK, WILDCAT and JOEY return to their seats.)

FRANK: Sorry, Billy. She meant well.

BILLY: *(Fighting not to cry again)* I'm so goddamn tired of everybody meaning well, and how they buy into that hero and thank-you-for-your-service crap.

(There is a prolonged pause, as though no one is certain what to say.)

WILDCAT: *(Looking suspiciously and hostilely at FRANK.)* Okay, we're alone now. Frank, what did you mean when you said Joey ruined your life?

FRANK: What the hell are you talking about?

WILDCAT: Just before Billy woke up. You said Joey ruined your life that day at Tri Binh. What were you talking about?

JOEY: Forget it, Wildcat. Let's just go into the kitchen, thank Betty for everything, and be on our way.

WILDCAT: No! We're still second squad. We have a right to know. What were you talking about, Frank? What did Joey do to you?

FRANK: I forget what I said.

WILDCAT: *(Stands, takes a couple steps toward FRANK.)* Goddamnit, you were pissed and looked at Joey like you wanted to kill him. Then you said he ruined your life.

BILLY: This is too heavy for me. Let's go. Now!

JOEY: Tri Binh messed up all of us, Wildcat. Tri Binh and lots of other places. *(Stands)* I'll go thank Betty for all of us, and then we ought to go.

WILDCAT: Goddamn it, Cherryboy! What did Joey do that Billy and me don't know about?

BILLY: *(Reaching for his canes and trying to stand)* I'm going outside. I need another hit.

JOEY: Just wait a second, Billy, and we'll all go to my car.

WILDCAT: *(His eyes remained fixed on* FRANK *while he angrily speaks to* BILLY.*)* Go ahead, Billy. Go waste yourself. The truth is nobody gives a rat's ass what you do.

BILLY: *(Screaming)* Incoming!

*(*BILLY *lurches forward and attempts to strike* WILDCAT *with a cane.* WILDCAT *jumps backwards and crashes into an end table. The lamp falls to the floor and shatters.* BILLY *falls face down with a loud thud.)*

JOEY: *(Steps quickly to* BILLY, *rolls him onto his back, and kneels beside him.)* Billy! Billy!

BETTY: *(Entering hurriedly from stage right, she sees* BILLY *and kneels beside* JOEY. *She begins sobbing.)* Why did I buy so much beer? This is all my fault, all my fault!

WILDCAT: *(Moving beside* BETTY*)* My fault, ma'am. My fault. Billy, I didn't mean it, man.

*(*BETTY *glances toward* FRANK *who remains seated:)*

BETTY: Frank! Help us, for God's sake! How can you just sit there?

FRANK: *(Sarcastically)* Want me to call a goddamn dustoff or something? *(Stands and joins the others.)* Looks like he's breathing okay.

BETTY: What the hell's wrong with you, Frank? Grab a pillow!

FRANK: *(Reaches for a sofa pillow and languidly hands it to* BETTY.*)* Here.

BETTY: *(Yanks the pillow from* FRANK*)* Can you lift your head, Billy?

BILLY: *(Raises his head slightly and allows* BETTY *to slip the pillow beneath him. His speech is strained and barely audible.)* I'm okay. No big deal.

JOEY: *(Slides both his arms under* BILLY*)* I'm going to carry you back over to the couch. Tell me if it hurts anywhere. *(He grunts as he lifts* BILLY. *He carries him to the sofa and gently lays him down. He grabs another pillow and props it under* BILLY's *head.)* You want a blanket?

BILLY: *(Shaking his head)* I'm okay.

WILDCAT: *(Moves beside* JOEY *and stands over* BILLY*)* I'm so sorry, man. I'm so sorry.

BETTY: I never should have bought so much beer.

JOEY: You've been wonderful, Betty. Billy will be fine. Just one of those things.

WILDCAT: *(Reflexively snapping to attention)* I'll pay for the lamp, ma'am. You just tell me where you bought it, and I'll get one just like it first thing in the morning.

BETTY: I don't care about the lamp.

*(*BETTY *turns angrily to* FRANK *who has returned to his recliner.)*

BETTY: All I care about is why my worthless husband just sat on his butt when Billy fell down. What kind of buddy are you, Frank? Is this the way he was in Vietnam, Joey? Wildcat? What kind of buddy thinks only of himself?

JOEY: Frank was always there for us, ma'am. Everything's okay.

WILDCAT: He was the best, ma'am. We were always there for each other. One time——

BETTY: *(Glaring at* FRANK*)* Look at him lying back in that chair with that big smirk on his face. I thought just once, just this one special time, he could drink with his old buddies and look what happens.

FRANK: *(Returns* BETTY's *glare for several seconds.)*

I never told you I wanted this so-called reunion.

BETTY: (Marches up to Frank, leans forward,

and slaps him hard.) You bastard.

WILDCAT: I think we better go, ma'am.

FRANK: *(Stands slowly, pauses before speaking antagonistically.)*

Gee, Wildcat, if you leave now you'll never know what Joey did to me at Tri Binh. What he did to all of us.

BETTY: I never should have let you drink today. You're an ass, Frank. It's embarrassing.

WILDCAT: *(Hostilely)* So what did he do, Frank? What the hell were you talking about?

FRANK: *(Nods toward* JOEY*)* You came here today just for this, didn't you, Hardrock? You never even knew I was alive until a few days ago, didn't think you'd ever see me again, thought you'd never have a chance to ask me to forgive you. Well, it's not going to happen!

WILDCAT: What the hell does he mean, Joey? Somebody talk!

JOEY: I was hoping to catch you alone, Frank, just the two of us. Never mind now. Billy, Wildcat, we can go now.

FRANK: You're not going anywhere, Hardrock! Tell all your old buddies here what really happened to Joker! We're all ears.

JOEY: You said before we all ate that nobody needed to know what happened at Tri Binh.

FRANK: I don't give a good goddamn what I said!

BILLY: What the hell are you two trying to do? Joker's gone and that's that. Leave him alone.

FRANK: *(Addressing* BETTY*)* You really want to know how your hero husband got wounded, my dear?

*(*BETTY*, aghast, backs slowly toward the rear wall, listening intently.)*

JOEY: This isn't necessary, Frank.

FRANK: It's as necessary as anything I've ever done! *(Again addresses* BETTY*.)* Okay, my princess, so you really want to know how I got wounded. In fact, everyone here got wounded at the same miserable time, the same miserable day. Right, Joey?

JOEY: You fool.

FRANK: The same day Joker got it. Right Joey?

JOEY: *(Resignedly)* As we all know.

FRANK: Well, my innocent spouse here doesn't know a thing about it because I've never told her what really happened. Never once in my pointless life have I told her. *(Laughing sardonically)* Maybe she thinks I got all these scars from my scalp to my heels when I got peppered with shrapnel from a Viet Cong RPG. Maybe she thinks I got hit charging through a rice paddy under heavy machine gun fire. Maybe she thinks I saved a couple lives even though I was bleeding all over myself. Who knows?

BILLY: *(Struggling to stand)* I don't have room for this. You guys are nuts. I'm going outside. *(Falls back onto the sofa.)* Fuck!

*(*WILDCAT *and* BILLY*, transfixed, remain focused on* FRANK *and* JOEY*.)*

FRANK: *(His voice rises as he addresses* BETTY*,* BILLY *and* WILDCAT*, ignoring* JOEY*.)* Joker was the only man I've

ever loved, and I'm not afraid to say it. No, not that
sick homo love, but a love deeper than two brothers.
I didn't know anything about Nam when I got there.
They told me I had to kill gooks before they could
destroy the good ole U S A. But Joker, he started
making me see the whole thing was bullshit. He got
me started on weed, and we started talking, talking
about everything. And one night on L Z Osage he told
me he was putting in for Australia for R and R. He
started laying it all out, how he wouldn't come back
to Nam, how he would hide in Australia and get a job.
And then how he'd start buying land for a sheep ranch,
starting small and building it up. And how he would
find cowgirls to work the ranch and make love to them.
It sounded crazy, but he kept it up and pretty soon I
started thinking he could do it. Maybe it was the weed.
Maybe it was just being out there in the boonies day
after day, night after night, getting shot at, gagging in
the heat, pulling leaches off each other's back, seeing
other guys in the platoon get their asses blown away.
But one night I told him he had the right idea and that,
by God, I would go with him. So we both put in for
Australia, and son-of-a-bitch if we didn't get it.

BILLY: Help me up, Wildcat. Get me out of here!

(*Everyone ignores* BILLY *while* FRANK *continues.*)

FRANK: And then came Tri Binh, two days before we
were supposed to hop on that freedom bird to Sydney.
(*Pauses and turns to* BETTY.) You really want to know
how I got my Purple Heart, how all us heroes you fed
tonight got their Purple Hearts?

(BETTY, *crying silently, can only bite her lip.*)

FRANK: We were coming up on this little village. Tri
Binh. We were supposed to check the hooches for
weapons, like we'd done a million times before. And

then a couple snipers opened up on us. *(Turns to* JOEY*)* Am I right, Joey? Am I leaving out anything?

JOEY: *(Slowly shakes his head)* Nope.

FRANK: You bet I haven't. And we all know what happened next. The dumbest second lieutenant in the history of the United States Army panicked. He'd been in Nam for a whole month and knew less than any of us. He started screaming for everyone to return fire. And then he grabbed the radio headset, called the fire direction center, and screamed into it that we were being overrun and needed artillery. First round H E, high explosive. Joker was on the ground right next to him, and kept yelling for him to calm down, that it was only a couple snipers and they'd already stopped firing and run off. Joey and I were right there next to them. Am I telling it right, Joey? You heard Joker, too, right, telling the lieutenant to cool it?

JOEY: Everything you say is true.

FRANK: And then here comes the artillery, three booms in the distance. Funny thing about artillery, Betty. You can hear it coming, and you can tell from the whooshing and the whining if it's going to fall short of you or pass over. Only we knew this time it was going to come down right on top of us. Stokely, the dumb bastard who couldn't even read a map, had given the wrong coordinates.

BILLY: *(Screams and tries again to stand before falling backwards onto the sofa.)* Somebody get me the hell out of this madhouse!

FRANK: *(Ignoring* BILLY*)* And what did Joker do, Joey? Tell us what Joker did. Tell us what Joker did that Billy and Wildcat don't know about because they were on the other side of a hooch and couldn't see us. But you saw it same as me, right Joey?

JOEY: (*Becoming angry himself*) Sure I saw it, Cherryboy.
Sure I saw it. Joker yelled for Lieutenant Stokely to
keep down, and threw himself on top of him. That
what you wanted me to tell everyone, Cherryboy?
How Joker threw himself on top of Stokely and saved
his life?

WILDCAT: (*Jumps up*) No way! No fucking way!

FRANK: Bingo! Right again, Joey. First round came
down right through the roof of the hooch and went
off inside it. The shrapnel came through the walls, and
that's what hit Wildcat and Billy and the other guys
even if Joey and I couldn't see them. The second round
came down on the far side of the ville, over by first
and third squads. The ground shook so hard I thought
my ribs would break. And then came that third round.
How close to us did it land, Joey? You're a smart guy.

JOEY: Forty feet, maybe.

FRANK: More like thirty. Hit a bunch of banana trees
just a little to our right, and that's when we got it,
Joey and me and the lieutenant, but mostly Joker. I
remember those big ass banana leaves spiraling down
on us like green propellers. I'd always thought artillery
shrapnel was just these little pieces about the size of a
domino, but some of them can be as big as a shingle,
like the one that was sticking out of Joker's side like a
cleaver. It would have hit Stockley if Joker hadn't been
on top of him. I remember reaching for it, how hot it
was, how I could hardly pull it out. You remember
seeing it, Joey?

JOEY: I just remember the blood.

(WILDCAT *suddenly grabs one of* BILLY's *canes, cocks it
like a baseball bat, and steps quickly toward* FRANK. JOEY
forcefully drives his shoulder into WILDCAT's *midsection,
and they fall together to the floor.* BETTY, *screaming, jumps
backwards away from them.*)

BETTY: *(Crying)* Stop it! Please stop it! Frank! Stop them!

(JOEY, atop WILDCAT, grasps him around his chest and squeezes until WILDCAT is motionless.)

JOEY: You okay, Wildcat?

WILDCAT: *(Nodding rapidly, exhausted)* I'm okay.

(JOEY helps WILDCAT to his feet. BETTY sobs, her face in her hands. FRANK hasn't moved. Neither has BILLY, though tears are running down his face.)

WILDCAT: *(Returns uneasily to the sofa and collapses. He laughs without conviction while struggling for breath.)* Man, I'm out of shape.

JOEY: *(Returns to his recliner)* Sorry, Wildcat. *(Turns to FRANK.)* You done? We'd all like to get to the motel.

WILDCAT: Hold on, Joey. Let's hear it, Frank. I'm not leaving until you finish whatever the hell you think you're trying to do.

FRANK: *(Spitefully)* Almost done.

BILLY: *(Hatefully)* I wish I'd never come here. I wish Wildcat had never found you.

FRANK: *(Turning to BILLY)* Billy, when Betty told me she'd seen Wildcat's email that went to the nursery, the first thing I thought of was I wish she hadn't. I was afraid it would turn into something like this. I didn't want to see you or anyone. That's the truth.

BILLY: Know what, Cherryboy? I don't give a rat's ass. It don't mean nothin'!

FRANK: Ha! The magic words! It don't mean nothin'. *(Points to BETTY)* For the benefit of my poor, lost wife number three, whenever we lost somebody over there we just wrapped him up in his poncho, threw his ugly dead ass onto the dustoff, and said, "It don't mean nothin'." And then we moved on to the next firefight.

Didn't give the sucker another thought. Why? Because it didn't mean nothin'.

BILLY: *(Yelling)* Roger that, ma'am! Nothin' meant nothin'! My legs didn't mean nothin'! My ball didn't mean nothin'! Joker didn't mean nothin'! Hell, we didn't mean nothin'!

FRANK: I didn't want to see you, Billy, because I knew nothing good would come of it. And then Betty told me Wildcat and you were coming, and then this morning Wildcat told me Joey was coming, like you guys thought you had a perfect right to trespass into my life again. I didn't want to see any of you bastards, especially Joey.

WILDCAT: Well, we're here now, goddamnit, what about Joey and Tri Binh? Talk!

JOEY: Don't say a fucking word, Frank, because I'm going to save you the trouble. *(Turns quickly and angrily toward* BILLY *and* WILDCAT.*)* Frank thinks I'm a murderer because… *(Pauses and swallows.)* Because I shot Joker. Yep, I…I killed him. And Frank saw me do it.

BILLY: Jesus Christ!

WILDCAT: *(Yelling)* You what?

JOEY: *(Defiantly)* You heard me. I killed him! Shot him and killed him.

WILDCAT: *(Again jumps to his feet and starts for* JOEY, *but halts abruptly as* JOEY *draws back a fist. He faces* FRANK.*)* Frank?

FRANK: You heard the man.

WILDCAT: *(Turns to* JOEY*)* Son-of-a-bitch! Why?

JOEY: *(Hesitates)* Because. He wanted me to and I loved him.

WILDCAT: (*Facing* FRANK) You saw Joey kill Joker and you never told anyone? You never had the guts…I hope both you bastards rot in hell!

FRANK: (*Nodding with smug exaggeration*) So do I.

BILLY: (*Struggling to stand, he falls back again.*) Goddamnit!

BETTY: (*Crying uncontrollably*) I am so sorry.

WILDCAT: (*Glances back and forth at* JOEY *and* FRANK, *uncertain what to do. He starts for the door.*) I'm outta' here!

JOEY: Just like that? You want to run out without hearing the rest of it? Coward!

(WILDCAT *charges* JOEY *with a guttural scream. He tackles* JOEY *and they fall to the floor entwined.* BILLY *continues crying and yelling, while* BETTY *shrieks.* FRANK *doesn't move but looks away while* WILDCAT *and* JOEY *grunt and exchange blows as they roll entangled on the floor.*)

BETTY: Frank! Stop them!

(FRANK *slowly rises and stands over* WILDCAT *and* JOEY *as they continue fighting.* JOEY *hits* WILDCAT *with a resounding punch to the face, and* WILDCAT *signals he wants no more.* JOEY *helps him to his feet. Both men are breathing heavily, and* WILDCAT *leans forward to catch his breath. He is bleeding from the nose, and the front of his shirt is ripped open.* JOEY *reaches to the floor for* WILDCAT's *cap and hands it to him.* WILDCAT *uses it to wipe his nose, then slowly returns to the sofa.* FRANK *returns to his recliner.* BETTY *hurriedly exits stage right and quickly returns with a towel which she uses to wipe* WILDCAT's *nose.*)

WILDCAT: (*Grabbing the towel and pressing it against his nose.*) I'm okay. I'm okay.

JOEY: *(Speaking while trying to catch his breath)* We can't
be doing stuff like this at our age. Sorry, Wildcat. And
I'm really sorry for you, Betty.

BETTY: *(Tearfully)* I never should have done this.

WILDCAT: Just tell me one thing, Joey. What do you
mean Joker wanted you to shoot him?

JOEY: Frank could tell you but I know he won't.
(Turning toward FRANK.*)* What's it like to hate a man for
more than fifty years? I guess it doesn't leave a lot of
time for much else.

(No one moves or says a word for as much as ten seconds.)

JOEY: *(Collapses into his recliner, and captures his breath
before speaking haltingly.)* After that third artillery round
came down on top of us, everybody was screaming
and trying to figure out if they were dead. I looked up
and saw the lieutenant roll out from under Joker. There
was blood all over the top of Joker's head and face. But
both his eyes were open. I could tell he knew exactly
what had happened to him. Frank was able to crawl up
to him and kneel over him. That right, Frank?

FRANK: I was right there with my buddy, goddamnit.

JOEY: Frank started yelling at Joker, and trying to wipe
the blood off his face, but it just kept coming. He was
yelling about how he and Joker had promised to go
to Australia together, get a sheep ranch, make love
to cowgirls and everything else you guys heard him
talking about tonight.

FRANK: Now that's a goddamn lie! I was telling him to
hang on!

WILDCAT: Let him talk, Frank!

JOEY: I crawled up next to you, Frank. Joker's face
was pretty much gone, and his crotch was ripped

completely open. There was nothing there. You saw it, too. Tell Billy and Wildcat you saw it, too.

FRANK: *(Shaking his head defiantly)* I was begging him to hang on! He would have made it!

JOEY: *(Facing* BILLY *and* WILDCAT*)* I don't know how long we stayed like that, kneeling over Joker. The lieutenant was thrashing around and maybe trying to say something but I couldn't tell. The artillery had made everybody deaf almost. All I could hear was the screaming. You were messed up, too, Frank. Your shirt was gone, and your back was nothing but black and red holes. But I could tell at least you were going to be okay.

*(*FRANK *starts to speak but catches himself.)*

WILDCAT: *(Angrily)* Something you want to say, Frank? It better not be bullshit!

*(*FRANK *slowly shakes his head.)*

JOEY: *(Pausing before he continues)* I pulled my shirt off and stuck it where Joker's crotch had been, but it didn't do any good. His eyes told me how much pain he was in. I don't have any idea how long it took, but somebody was able to call a dustoff. I remember that chopper circling over us. Its shadow was moving back and forth over Joker's face. *(Looks directly at* FRANK*)* Joker started staring straight at you, Frank, begging you with his eyes for you to do it.

FRANK: Bullshit!

JOEY: Jesus, man! His entire manhood was gone, all ripped away like a buzzsaw had gone through him. His legs were hanging by the skin. And he knew it! He was begging you! Your buddy was begging you, Frank! He absolutely did not want to be thrown onto that dustoff alive. You knew it and I knew it.

FRANK: You lying, murdering bastard!

JOEY: I waited for you to do it, Frank. So help me, I waited for Joker's buddy to do what he wanted you to do. But all you could do was scream about Australia. So Joker looked over at me, and I nodded to let him know…to let him know that I would do it.

BILLY: *(Screaming and pounding the sofa)* Somebody get me the hell out of here!

JOEY: He was still able to mumble. Remember what he said, Frank? I know you read his lips just like I did.

FRANK: The man never said a thing. He was just waiting for us to carry him to the dustoff.

JOEY: I got down real close to him. He said… He said… You know what he said! You can still hear him just like I hear him everyday and every night. He said, "This is gonna' fuck up my mother." That's what he said! And then I stuck my M-16 into his mouth and…well, that was that.

(BILLY screams again, rolls onto the floor, and begins pounding it. BETTY cries and steps quickly to BILLY. WILDCAT intentionally falls onto Billy, and struggles to grab his flailing arms. JOEY hesitates, then drops to his knees to assist WILDCAT. FRANK starts to stand, but falls backward into his recliner. Finally, WILDCAT and JOEY carry BILLY, still screaming, to the sofa where WILDCAT hugs him tightly. BETTY, crying and standing nearby, is uncertain what to do.)

WILDCAT: *(Scowling at JOEY while squeezing BILLY)* Nice going, killer!

JOEY: *(Backing away, obviously horrified, more at himself than BILLY's reaction to what he has just said.)* Oh, God.

WILDCAT: *(Squeezing and rocking BILLY)* Billy, Billy. I love you, Billy. No matter what, Billy.

JOEY: *(Backing into his recliner)* Oh, Jesus God.

BILLY: (BILLY, *addressing* JOEY *while* WILDCAT *continues hugging him:*)

BILLY: I wish you'd killed me, too!

BETTY: Say something, Frank! Damn you, say something!

FRANK: (*He slowly surveys each of his guests in turn, then* BETTY, *lowers his face. He is subdued, his voice barely audible.*) I...I...I should have done it myself.

WILDCAT: You should have done it yourself? What the hell?

FRANK: (*Hesitating, struggling not to cry, his face still lowered*) I failed my buddy. (*Pausing*) And now I want to die.

(BETTY, *crying softly, moves to* FRANK's *side and tenderly but uncertainly takes his hand.*)

JOEY: (*Pauses, shakes his head*) I told myself on the drive up here that I wasn't going to say anything about Tri Binh. Nobody failed anybody, Frank.

(BILLY *slowly rolls out of* WILDCAT's *grasp and sits upright. There is a prolonged silence.*)

WILDCAT: You guys should have told somebody. The battalion commander, maybe. Not the part about what Joey did, but at least how the man saved Lieutenant Stockley's life. For God's sake, he did something none of us would have ever had the guts to do. He should... he should have got something. I mean, you're talking Medal of Honor stuff. I'm really pissed at both you guys.

JOEY: I don't blame you, Wildcat. I've never told a soul until now. I've always told myself it never happened.

WILDCAT: The man deserved something! Jesus.

FRANK: (*Looking toward the ceiling*) I was his buddy. I should have told somebody. I tell Joker everyday I should have told somebody something. I talk to Joker everyday. Sometimes when I'm driving I just start talking to him. Out loud, I mean. Sometimes I ask him how things are going on the ranch in Australia. And I always…always tell him how sorry I am I'm not there with him.

JOEY: I talk to Joker, too. I keep thinking it'll help me start living a normal life. I just want a normal life.

FRANK: *(Shakes his head slowly)* My life has been a total waste.

BETTY: *(Squeezing FRANK's hand.)* Oh, Frank.

BILLY: *(Letting out an exaggerated laugh)* Not as big a waste as mine.

WILDCAT: I guess all our lives have been a waste.

BETTY: Stop it, all of you!

JOEY: *(Exhausted, he lets out a deep breath and slowly stands.)* We need to go, guys. My car.

BILLY: Damn straight!

(BILLY reaches to the floor and fumbles for his canes. He tries to stand, then gives up. WILDCAT, not moving, glances alternately at FRANK and JOEY.)

WILDCAT: Wait a minute. Something's screwed up. I don't see how we can all just say goodnight. Not like this. Something ain't right.

(There is another lengthy pause. JOEY returns to his recliner. He, FRANK and WILDCAT look at each other for direction, while BILLY stares at the floor.)

JOEY: I agree. I need to say something to Frank. You were right about me coming here and hoping you'd forgive me. I was wrong to think like that. We were just kids and something happened to us. We just did what we thought we had to do. We're not bad people.

(Pauses and tears up again.) Seeing you guys today has meant the world to me.

BETTY: *(Wipes her face and tries to smile. She squeezes FRANK's shoulders.)* I know my husband doesn't say much but I know he feels the same way.

WILDCAT: *(Tearing up as well but trying to laugh.)* Look at us. I bet Joker would say we're just a bunch of pitiful crybabies.

JOEY: Billy, I know we all said it over there. "It don't mean nothin." But—

BILLY: None of it meant a damn thing! Jesus, we lost the fucking war! Or didn't you know, dumbass?

JOEY: *(Soothingly)* We're still second squad, Billy, like Wildcat said. That will always mean something.

BILLY: Your head's screwed up.

JOEY: We got as close over there as any group of guys could ever get. We weren't fighting for America, we were fighting for each other, looking out for each other. Other guys in second squad died for us, and we would have died for them. That's what Joker was doing when he saved Lieutenant Stokley. It meant something, Billy. It still means something or we wouldn't be here!

WILDCAT: *(Shaking his head)* But you killed Joker. How the hell can say you were looking out for him?

FRANK: *(Jumps to his feet.)* But Joey was looking out for him, goddamnit! He was looking out for Joker because I wasn't looking out for him. If Joker had lived he wouldn't have even been a man, just a blob. Joker knew it. Actually, Joey saved Joker!

WILDCAT: *(Again shaking his head)* I can't take anymore of this.

FRANK: Wildcat, you told me this morning it sounded crazy but the happiest you've ever been was when we were second squad in Nam. That's because it meant something, as screwed up as it was.

BILLY: You said that, Wildcat? You actually said that?

WILDCAT: Yeah. I said that.

BILLY: Then you're batshit.

FRANK: It was you, Wildcat, who carried Billy here to the dustoff, in bad a shape as you were in spite of Joey's tourniquet. Don't tell me that didn't mean nothin'.

(FRANK slowly returns to his recliner. The men take their time looking at each other.)

WILDCAT: I don't know if I could ever see how Nam meant something. Joey, does your grandson say getting screwed up in Afghanistan means something?

JOEY: *(Pauses)* He's coming along. And he still hears from his buddies. That helps a lot.

(There is another extended silence before WILDCAT speaks.)

WILDCAT: Know what, guys? I'm really tired. The food was great, Betty.

BETTY: *(Nodding with a smile)* You're welcome back anytime. I want you all to know that.

JOEY: We're all tired. *(Stands)* The motel's not that far. You're wonderful, Betty.

WILDCAT: *(Also stands)* Yes, ma'am. That steak beat the hell out of any c-rations I ever had.

BILLY: *(Reaches for his canes, but WILDCAT instead hoists him and lifts him onto his back.)* Heh, this is how you carried me to the dustoff.

WILDCAT: *(Speaking over his shoulder)* Just taking care of my buddy. We'll always be buddies, Billy.

(JOEY picks up BILLY's canes. JOEY and WILDCAT, with BILLY on his back, gather at the front door. BETTY joins

them, and repeatedly hugs each one. FRANK *finally joins them and does the same.)*

BILLY: *(Laughing)* We look like a bunch of queers.

WILDCAT: *(Suddenly enthusiastic)* Heh, I just got a great idea. You know what we ought to do? We should drive all the way to Washington, DC, and go see that wall. We should find Joker's name and…and touch it. We should leave something for him. Hell, we ought to leave our Purple Hearts with him, right under his name. I've seen them do it on T V. Heh, that would mean something!

JOEY: Hell, yes!

WILDCAT: We could touch him and talk to him all we want. I wouldn't give a good goddamn who heard us.

JOEY: I'll foot for the rooms. Hell, yes!

WILDCAT: Billy?

BILLY: Why should I go see that black slit trench after my own country tied to kill me? I trashed my medals long ago.

WILDCAT: You're coming with us whether you like it or not. Cherryboy, anything holding you back?

FRANK: I'd have to think about it.

BETTY: *(Gripping* FRANK *around the waist)* I'll make sure he thinks about it.

JOEY: Then it's a deal.

*(*JOEY *holds open the door and stands aside while* WILDCAT *carries* BILLY *outside. He faces* FRANK *and* BETTY*.)*

JOEY: I think it would be best if we just headed on back to Oklahoma in the morning, but I'll make sure we all stay in touch. We're going to go see Joker, by God. *(Nods goodbye.)* Night.

BETTY: Goodnight, second squad.

(JOEY *exits and* BETTY *closes the door. She attempts to hug* FRANK, *but he turns away and returns to his recliner.*)

FRANK: Sorry. I just need to sit.

BETTY: *(Standing beside him)* I know the day didn't go the way you expected, but—

FRANK: *(Defensively)* I always told you I wasn't a war hero. Wrong place, wrong time. That's all I ever said. And now you know. Friendly fire, they called it. Friendly fucking fire.

BETTY: Why didn't you tell me all this when we started getting serious? It wouldn't have made any difference to me. You could have at least told me about Joker. You had someone like that in your life and you couldn't even tell me?

FRANK: Robert Metz. His real name was Robert Metz. He was from Pine Bay, Florida, and his birthday was June 7.

BETTY: My God. The same as yours.

FRANK: He was a year older than me.

BETTY: *(Shakes her head)* Are you happy here, Frank? I mean, happy with me, your kids, everything else? You're just so distant sometimes. A lot of the time, actually. You said some awful things about me tonight, and didn't help us when Billy fell.

FRANK: *(Shrugs)* Sorry. Sometimes...sometimes I don't feel things.

BETTY: I make you angry, don't I, Frank? You look at me and you get angry because you're not in Australia on your ranch with Joker.

FRANK: *(Deliberates before answering)* It's not you. It's the whole thing. This house, this town, my whole damn life. *(Pauses, trying to contain himself.)* It's Nam and I can't stop it. Joker and I were dreaming.

BETTY: What can I do?

FRANK: I don't know. Just promise me Rob and Cindy will never know what happened that day, even after I'm dead.

BETTY: No. You need to tell them yourself someday. You need to tell them, and they need to hear it from you. *(Moves to where she can face FRANK)* You need to go see that wall with your buddies.

FRANK: I can't think about it right now.

BETTY: Then take a few days and think about it. I wouldn't dare think of going with you if that's what you're worried about.

FRANK: *(Stands and awkwardly grabs BETTY around the waist. He looks into her face, then lowers his. He hesitates.)* I'm so sorry for what I said about you. I 'm, well, really screwed up.

BETTY: *(Places an open hand under FRANK's jaw and lifts his face to hers.)* We'll work on it.

(FRANK eases into his recliner while sliding his hands down to BETTY's hips. He buries his face into her abdomen and begins shaking uncontrollably.)

BETTY: *(Stroking FRANK's head, she speaks softly.)* Welcome home, Cherryboy.

(Blackout)

(End of scene)

(Curtain)

END OF PLAY